FROM HEART AND SOUL

A Collection of Poems

John Marshall

John Marshall

Published by Saron Publishing in 2018

Copyright © 2018 John Marshall

All rights reserved

No part of this publication may be reproduced, stored in a retrieval system, or transmitted, in any form or by any means, without the prior permission in writing of the publisher, nor be otherwise circulated in any form of binding or cover other than that in which it is published and without a similar condition including this condition being imposed on the subsequent purchaser

ISBN-13: 978-0-9956495-9-0

Saron Publishing
Pwllmeyrick House
Mamhilad
Mon
NP4 8RG

saronpublishers.co.uk
Follow us on Facebook or Twitter

The author is donating all profits from this book to Cancer Research

John Marshall

DEDICATION

This collection of poems is dedicated to all those who have, over the years, supported and encouraged my love of poetry. The English language has always been very special to me, and to a large extent this is due to my parents, Stan and Marjorie, who always encouraged me to read a wide and diverse range of books.

On reaching high school, this interest was reinforced by my English language and literature teacher, Miss Blyth, who was of the 'old school', encouraging all her students to use language creatively, and explore all forms of literature. It was under her tutelage that I first started to pen my own poetry.

However, the greatest credit goes to my beloved wife, Dot, who was not only appreciative of my efforts, but also, as will be seen from the more 'personal' items included here, became a great source of inspiration. I would add at this point that she is aware of, and in agreement with, their inclusion!

John Marshall

ACKNOWLEDGEMENTS

In addition to the comments in the preceding dedication, I would also like to thank Dot for helping me proof read the contents, and also acknowledge the great encouragement, help and support I have received from Saron Publishers in the preparation for publication of this collection.

John Marshall

CONTENTS

1	A Forever Love	11
2	A Pastoral Poem	12
3	Solitary Confinement	15
4	Robin	16
5	Your Love Is My Life	18
6	Why?	19
7	Creature of the Night	21
8	Paper Preferences	22
9	Tunisian Love	23
10	Ten By Ten	24
11	Sea-Scape	26
12	The Dream	27
13	Libby	28
14	Libby	29
15	A Jubilee Walk	31
16	Compromise	33
17	Cage Bird	34
18	Dad	36
19	The Cess Pit	37
20	Living Life	38
21	The Love Tree	39
22	Time Warp	41
23	The Tragedy That is War	42
24	Bing The Magnificent	44
25	The Black and White Minstrel Show	46
26	The Old Man	48
27	Motorway Meetings	49
28	The Oak Tree	51
29	These Things You Are	52
30	The N.H.S.	53
31	Our Fate-Full Lives	55
32	Poppies	56
33	The Graceful Swan	57

John Marshall

34	Now and Forever	58
35	If Heaven Had a Telephone	59
36	A Gentle Word	60
37	Dreams	61
38	Love In My Heart	62
39	The Dragon Slayer	63
40	Forgetting To Remember	71
41	Love Is The Greatest Feeling	72
42	A Flight From Nowhere	73
43	Tunnel Terrorism	75
44	Love As Art Displayed	77
45	The Eternal Moon	79
46	Love Defined	80
47	What Is Love?	81
48	The Value of Independence	83

FROM HEART AND SOUL

A FOREVER LOVE

I did not meet you when we met -
For I had known you long ago.
We had not been together, yet
Our Love was there, that much I know.

I have known your Love since I was born,
As you were aware of mine.
I knew our Love had been foresworn,
And that we would share our lives, sometime.

I dreamed of us throughout my life,
Though not knowing if we'd meet.
But now, my dear, we are man and wife,
Our Love and Lives complete.

I have loved you long, and forever will;
 I bless the day we met.
I will Love you until our hearts are still,
And will Love you longer yet.

John Marshall

A PASTORAL POEM

Words depicting the themes and content of Beethoven's Symphony No 6 (Pastoral), a personal favourite since primary school days. Many thanks to my parents for encouraging my love of all good music, but especially Classical.

I leave the grime, the smoke and the noise behind -
All the pollution involved with modern life.
I search for the tranquility I keep in my mind
As an antidote to Humanity's grief and strife.

As the buildings recede, and the countryside nears,
Dark thoughts and Life's problems fade away.
Gone are job worries, and associated fears,
My soul is at home, where it yearns to stay.

Fields of corn sway and dance to an unheard song,
And splashes of colour re-educate my sight.
Happiness returns, having been absent too long,
As I see Nature in all her majestic, beautiful might.

I follow the lane, as it winds its way,
Intoxicated by sights and smells all around,
Until I reach a bridge, with a brook at play,
Chuckling at some private joke - such a cheerful sound!

It stretches away on either hand;
Reeds and grasses adorn its flanks,
Hiding the boundary 'twixt water and land
Between and amongst their serried ranks.

FROM HEART AND SOUL

The water gurgles and glides in its rocky bed -
Crystal clear, and yet flecked with foam.
Apparently aimless, it surges ahead,
As if its only purpose is to wander and roam.

The sound of voices floats on the air,
Music and singing entwined, hand in hand.
A corner discloses a bright country fair,
With locals enjoying a small village band.

Twisting and swirling their rustic dance
In celebration of the harvest complete,
Costumed Morris-men jump and prance,
With streamers and bells on hands and feet.

But dark clouds gather and form overhead,
And the air becomes oppressive and still.
The villagers, once joyful, become quiet instead,
As the clouds begin their burden to spill.

The sky is rent with flashes of light,
And jagged, fiery spears skewer sky to ground.
Animals scatter in confusion and fright
As the thunder booms and echoes around.

Then, as it started, the storm quickly goes.
The clouds disperse, and the sun re-appears.
With a few final rumblings, the storm's death-throes
Are greeted by choruses of laughter and cheers.

A single melodic flute begins to play,
Stark contrast to the storm's anger and noise,
A shepherd is saying thank-you, in his own simple way,
As life returns to its usual calm and poise.

John Marshall

The storm, though violent, is part of one vast Plan,
Enabling life's cycle to begin again,
Harvested and channeled with the aid of Man,
Nature will harness and use the sun and rain.

I continue my walk, peace all around me once more;
My mind refreshed, my spirit renewed.
At one with Nature, as never before,
My feelings with rural simplicity imbued.

FROM HEART AND SOUL

SOLITARY CONFINEMENT

Awareness – that wondrous gift of the human brain;
Ephemeral, indefinable, but present from birth to death.
The power to think and act, given to the healthy and the sane;
Accepted, but unappreciated, along with each unconscious breath.

Imagine then, the isolation of the artist, suddenly blind;
or the musician, unable to hear;
the orator, unable to speak his mind –
the change from sensory awareness to confusion and fear.

Think of the indignity and distress that senility brings –
The questioning eyes striving to understand;
Demeaned by insanity and personality swings;
The mind no longer in command.

Empathise with the victim of paralysis,
Whose mind is still fully aware –
Unable to communicate their life in crisis,
Immobile, frustrated, helpless, in despair.

How irreplaceable are those cells within our head,
Which give choice to what we think and do.
How frightening, should those cells become our prison, instead –
Solitary confinement, with no hope of a Judicial Review.

John Marshall

ROBIN

Robin looked down from his comfy bush,
and saw a man he did not know.
He was digging away, without any rush,
working steadily, down below.

Robin had seen men many times before
as he watched their movements with care -
but of any danger he was still unsure,
and was wary to approach when Man was there.

Robin watched Man regularly, curiosity sparked,
and his confidence slowly grew.
His understanding of Man became more marked,
and his approaches to the man began anew.

There came the day when Man spotted Robin there,
and Man's interest was aroused as well.
The two of them, Robin and Man, were both aware
of the other's interest, and mutual trust began to swell.

As man was digging, he found a worm,
and took it from the ground.
He held it out, and Robin watched it squirm
and, appetite whet, he looked around.

No danger there was he able to see,
and so flew down and landed close to Man.
The worm was thrown - a juicy delicacy,
which Robin took and ate with great elan.

FROM HEART AND SOUL

From that moment, the friendship flourished -
Man and Robin now sought to seal the tie.
To understand each other was what they wished,
and they asked themselves 'How?' not 'Why?'

Finally, that physical contact was achieved,
as Robin settled on Man's outstretched hand.
Neither found that their trust was deceived,
and their relationship progressed as planned.

Robin had often heard the sounds that Man made,
but had no understanding of what they were.
Now, with that touch, their meaning displayed
the communication that they had to share.

From that day forward their thoughts they shared,
and true friendship between them flourished.
They understood each other, and each one cared
what the other liked and wished.

And now, wherever a man is on his land,
tending his crops, and digging the ground,
a red breast robin will be found, close at hand –
when one is there, the other will surely be around!

John Marshall

YOUR LOVE IS MY LIFE

A gentle word like a spark of light
Illuminates my soul;
And as each sound goes deeper,
It's you that makes me whole.

There is no corner, no dark place,
Your LOVE cannot fill;
And if the world starts causing waves,
It's your devotion that makes them still.

And yes, you always speak to me
In sweet honesty and truth;
Your caring heart keeps out the rain,
Your LOVE the ultimate roof.

So thank you, my LOVE, for being there,
For supporting me, my life;
I'll do the same for you, you know,
My beautiful, Darling Wife.

FROM HEART AND SOUL

WHY?

On a clear Spring night,
under a bright, starlit sky,
I look on Nature's might,
and I ask the question – WHY?

Why, out of all the stars on parade,
many, no doubt, with a circling world,
Should our Sun put the rest in shade
with our Planet, her beauty unfurled?

Why, once our gem was formed,
and the flora and fauna released,
why then, was Mankind ever spawned
to ruin our planet, and leave it diseased?

Why, when his intellect knows no bound,
should he choose to spoil his home? –
to kill, to maim, to poison the ground,
and imprison life that was once free to roam?

Why does man alone choose to kill his own kind
for reasons no more than pure pleasure?
Why should Man's questing, questioning mind
possess evil in equal measure?

Why cannot Man learn to respect all life –
on land, in the air, and the seas?
Why must man cause perpetual strife
And bring the World crashing to its knees?

John Marshall

Why, when some can see the trend
Cannot the madness be stopped?
Why can no-one start to mend,
And re-plant, where once trees were cropped?

Before long, it will be too late,
And the chances will be long since gone?
Man will be left to follow his fate
On a barren, lifeless World, ALONE!

WHY?????????????????????????????

FROM HEART AND SOUL

CREATURES OF THE NIGHT

Inspired by a quiet night shift driving in the beautiful rural Sussex countryside.

Man is not nocturnal by habit, or desire.
As a rule, his nights are spent asleep.
His world ends when he chooses to retire,
Ignorant of the wondrous company he declines to keep.

The rabbit, ever alert, with ears held aloft,
Trimming roadside verges, pastureland and park.
Fleeing suddenly, his wave goodbye a fluffy tuft
As he scurries for anonymity in the dark.

The fox, his eyes on fire in a car's bright light,
His trotting walk full of purpose and poise.
Just a fleeting glimpse as he disappears in fright,
Alert and suspicious of the slightest noise.

Brock the badger, in his evening suit,
Always bumbling along with that curious gait.
Undeviating, unwavering in his choice of route,
Always in a hurry, seemingly always late.

The hunting owl, a soundless, deadly blur,
Glimpsed briefly as he floats and soars –
His sharp eyes register a flurry of fur
And he strikes and kills, with razor claws.

Of all these creatures man is unaware
As he sleeps his way through every night.
How sad that he should not be there
When nature displays her nocturnal might.

John Marshall

PAPER PREFERENCES

Tabloids and broadsheets come and go,
Collected, or delivered, as preference dictates.
An individual's choice may unintended show
more secrets than the name first indicates.

Watch out for the lady's choice,
as she calls in each day, without fail –
the flashing eyes, the breathy voice,
as she ensures she collects her *Daily Mail*.

Beware the stunning page three dish,
Though for some conjuring up images of heaven.
Lest you, like Icarus, fall and perish
Through over-exposure to *The Sun*.

Identify with the more discerning reader,
Who seeks a journal he feels will impress.
He fancies himself as some 'caped crusader'
As he poses proudly with his *Daily Express*.

No prizes for guessing the Party this customer chooses;
Not for him the trivia of the common herd.
Daily, work-bound, he sits and muses
Over *The Telegraph*'s cryptic crossword.

The newsagent sees them come and go,
Like snapshots, showing the diversity of reading choice –
Privy to the reader's habits, he is in the know
As to their preference of Media voice.

FROM HEART AND SOUL

TUNISIAN LOVE

One of the many of these poems written for my wife…this one after we had a holiday in Tunisia.

You are the most beautiful thing in the world to me,
No matter when, or where we are.
No difference, in Birmingham or La Tunisie,
Or whether we travel near or far.

Your fair shining tresses hang free and loose,
Cascading round your slender neck;
Shining as the sun on the Medina in Sousse,
Blowing in the wind, as the sails of a chebec.

Your look radiates the Love you give to me,
As you gaze with longing upon my face –
I need not visit Port Al Kantoui,
For your Love is with me, in every place.

No matter the hour, it is with me yet,
Forever blessing me with its grace.
From Port Tunis, as far as Hammamet,
It is with me, eternally, where ere the place.

No Arab Souk, or market square
Can sell that with which we are possessed –
For wherever we are, our Love is there –
It is strongest in us, and outshines the rest.

John Marshall

TEN BY TEN

Measurements used to vary from state to state,
with different countries using different rules.
Acre, chain, furlong, pound, stone and hundredweight,
yard, foot and inch are what we learned in schools.

Farthing, halfpenny, penny, sixpence and shilling –
florin, half crown, crown, and pound.
So much school-time, with schoolteachers instilling
their charges with a knowledge that had to be sound.

How complicated it all seemed to be,
as we struggled to make those numbers stick –
imperial measurements were the norm for you and me,
times tables up to TWELVE? - it made me sick!

But what option was there, in our day?
We were British, so we had no choice.
But then Europeans started to have their say,
and common sense started to raise its voice.

Multiples of ten – that was the choice,
whether volume, currency, distance or weight.
'It will be so much easier,' said the voice
of reason, as it entered the debate.

Of course, reason won the day,
as the common market loomed.
Decimalisation, of course, was here to stay,
and Imperial measurement was doomed!

FROM HEART AND SOUL

But how would we cope with so much change?
Would we adapt to what was ahead?
Would our brain cells re-arrange?
And if not, what was there instead?

By and large, things worked out well,
as we adapted to something beyond our ken.
Our fears of change began to dispel,
and we slowly accepted 'ten by ten'.

John Marshall

SEA-SCAPE

A picture on my lounge wall in the 1990s, in line of sight many hours daily.

A leaden sky clothed in scudding clouds,
with rays of sunshine battling through;
curtains of rain, hanging in misty shrouds,
seeking to hide the ocean below from view.

Waves crashing against a rocky shore,
pushing columns of spray to meet the rain;
surging, rushing, then receding once more,
before gathering the strength to return again.

Seagulls, banking and soaring in the turbulent sky,
as they strive to conquer the air –
the most acrobatic, yet graceful, of all that fly –
with land, sea and air their lives they share.

The dunes of sand and grass stand fast,
though attacked by the salt, wind and spray –
shifting, bending, until the storm has passed;
constantly changing and moving, both determined to stay.

Islands and rocks peer out of the murk,
as the rain squalls pass them by.
Defiant witnesses to all of nature's work;
Solid, unyielding, lasting to eternity.

The unimaginable power of sea and sky –
A challenge thrown down to Man.
To live with them both we will always try,
But to master them? We never can!

FROM HEART AND SOUL

THE DREAM

Written after a particularly vivid nightmare, the content of which is obvious from the content of the poem.

My dream finds me in the killing fields
created by Bosnia's war and strife –
where love, and reason, and humanity, yields
to the conflict's continual need for taking life.

Bullet after bullet burrow deep into my skin,
and my life-blood begins to leak and drain:
Impact after impact, more than I can imagine,
And yet, surprisingly, I feel no pain.

I am aware that my future is drifting away,
And yet all seems calm and tranquil.
But I sense that there is so much that I need to say
Before my heart finally empties, and lies forever still.

Friends to see, to whom I need to explain
So many things, as yet unsaid –
Those people who I will never see again,
But whose memories I keep intact inside my head.

And, at last, in my head, I talk with *you*,
As I approach my journey's end.
I share my thoughts with a friend so true –
it is with you my final moments I choose to spend.

John Marshall

LIBBY

Tribute to our pet dog who passed away in 2014

Our beloved Libby has passed away
To that Battersea Dogs home in the sky -
We miss her more than words can say,
But our memories make us smile, not cry.

She will sniff until the clouds run dry -
All animals will be her friend.
With wings, once more she will freely fly
Until to her bed she will sleepily descend.

'Bat-ears', and 'Heavy-lump' are names she knows,
'Trouble' and 'Cheeky girl' too!
We will remember her with a fragrant rose,
A loving reminder for me and you.

FROM HEART AND SOUL

LIBBY

The Laughing Dog is now at rest;
amongst all dogs, the best of the best.
With a heart of gold, a friend to all,
she related to animals both large and small.

A 'Battersea dog' who won over our heart,
she charmed our lives from the very start.
When young, her energy knew no bounds,
and she was keen to explore all sights and sounds.

Long walks and bike rides were her norm;
a bundle of energy wrapped in a beautiful form.
With nose to the ground she sniffed her way,
always happy to run and play.

As 'gypsy dog' she toured near and far,
happy on our 'bus', or in the car.
Passport to paw, ready to explore,
she crossed our land from shore to shore.

Abroad, she explored pastures new,
happy to find new things to do,
loving to swim in the River Rhine,
and diving in the sea from time to time.

At home, canal cycle rides had a regular place,
and her pleasure showed in the smile on her face.
An occasional unexpected canal-side bath
resulted in a sheepish, embarrassed laugh.

John Marshall

In the car, she sat and looked, as if the Queen,
and watched the world pass by, all seen.
Often standing between us, looking ahead,
as if she would prefer to drive, instead.

Although happy wherever she might be,
the garden was her own special territory.
The first thing she did when returning home
was to pay a visit, and reclaim her own.

Night-time excursions were a regular thing,
when she sought to meet what the dark would bring
foxes, yes, and cats, maybe –
but we were never sure of what she would see.

So much joy she brought our way,
filling our lives with pleasure, day by day.
Memories flood wherever we are –
memories of our baby, no longer there.

Libby, we give our thanks for the times we knew,
for the fun and pleasure we had with you –
you will always have a place in our heart,
and our memories ensure we are never apart.

FROM HEART AND SOUL

A JUBILEE WALK

Written to commemorate a 1998 walk on the South Downs in Sussex, around Lewes, organised by Sussex Police to celebrate the 30th anniversary of the amalgamation of various Police Forces in Sussex into the Sussex Police. During my latter years of service in that Force, I ran a unit of Police Cadets, based at Rye, and the unit and I took part as a group. We all finished, and I still have the medal!!!

The walkers stand, the event awaits;
supressed energy and excitement fill the air;
The experienced, and otherwise, contemplate their fates,
mindful of the challenge they are about to share.

The moment arrives, and participants depart,
as varied a group as you could wish to get.
Mr Blobby, policemen and their families leave the start –
Prison officers, civilians, friends, and even the odd energetic pet!

A crisp autumn morning sees them on their way,
striding purposefully out onto The Downs.
With the promise of fine weather throughout the day,
Lewes emerges from the mist, like a jewelled crown.

Downland, valleys, tracks and roads
all pass with the miles, beneath their feet,
and with the final steep climb, the vista explodes
on their senses, dispelling all thoughts of defeat.

As the day progresses, many battles are fought –
Individuals, determined to fight through their pain,
Struggling onward, with the one over-riding thought –
to finish, aware of the satisfaction they have to gain.

John Marshall

Groups build, disperse, and re-group once more;
all who are able seek to help and encourage another -
those who have flagged, they seek to restore,
and bonds are formed as if sister and brother.

The goal in sight, with thoughts of prizes around their necks,
they seek to find that last, long-hidden reserve,
and make the final, most important, uphill trek
to accept the reward they so richly deserve.

Personal achievement and friendship are also a gift to <u>all</u>,
not just to those who managed to complete the course.
Thank you to all for taking part, answering the call,

AND FOR CELEBRATING THIS MILESTONE FOR OUR SUSSEX FORCE.

FROM HEART AND SOUL

COMPROMISE

Life is a compromise, rarely achieved,
with the balance of things never quite found:
Common sense ignored, intentioned deceived;
intended choices running hard aground.

Life is a compromise from beginning to end,
and ceaseless striving to make things balance –
one alternative seeking to contend
with the other, opposing, stance.

Human nature will never settle for one point of view,
although simplicity is all that is required;
instead, we look for alternatives anew
until we have to settle for the final compromise – life expired.

John Marshall

CAGE BIRD

Imprisoned behind bars, its soul confined,
Captured by boring routine for all eternity –
trapped by the cage, alone with its mind,
sentenced to a life of mediocrity.

Able to look out on the world beyond,
with only the chance to dream of flight –
only in its thoughts able to abscond,
lost in daydreams, alone every night.

Considered by many to be a beautiful thing,
a possession to be admired –
Lavished with praises that have a hollow ring,
Its captivity the evil in which they all conspired.

No hope of any last-minute reprieve;
no chance of freedom, of life anew.
But all the time in the world to ponder, and grieve
for the pleasure it once knew.

Then, without warning, that moment is there,
so unexpected as to be almost ignored.
A door is opened, and left unattended,
leaving freedom beckoning, and a life restored.

Once released, the bird takes flight,
and soars on high, its joy unbounded.
But yet, that freedom brings with it fright;
In uncertainty and disbelief it become surrounded.

FROM HEART AND SOUL

Is the release and freedom here to stay?
Or will captivity return once more?
It would hurt more that words could ever say
to return to the life it had grown to deplore.

John Marshall

DAD

Tribute to my dad read by me at his funeral.

You have been in my life from my earliest days -
a solid foundation for my life ahead.
You were there for me in so many ways,
never condemning, but supportive instead.

When I needed a friend, you were there,
solidly by my side.
When I needed help my load to bear,
your support you would always provide.

Moral guidance you would always give,
And teach me wrong from right –
show me the proper way to live,
to be honest, truthful and polite.

You loved good music, the first I heard,
A gift that will stay forever.
A love of reading, and the written word,
To amuse me through life's bad weather.

But most of all you gave me Love,
never cloying, or restricting, but always there.
Now you and Mum are re-united up above,
together in eternity, your time to share.

Forever in our hearts we hold a place for you,
giving thanks for the times we've had –
our memories of you will be forever true,
making us happy, thoughtful, but never sad.

FROM HEART AND SOUL

THE CESS-PIT

after saying there wasn't ANYTHING I couldn't write a poem about, I accepted a challenge to write about a cess-pit (an emptying tanker had just driven past us)

Malodourous, much maligned,
they hide themselves secretly away –
basic, functional, unrefined,
yet, it seems destined to stay.

Indispensable, many would say;
indefensible, to many others,
as the lingering, cloying bouquet
all other senses smothers.

Their contents, unwanted waste;
an embarrassing problem product.
A topic ignored, or discussed with haste,
a subject deliberately overlooked.

Cess-pits, sewers, or septic tanks –
we all have need of such things.
Be grateful for them all, and give thanks
for the sanitary service that each brings!

John Marshall

LIVING LIFE

When you feel that life is full of difficulties and problems,
remember that the <u>first</u> problem is to decide <u>which</u> life?
The real one, that you experience,
or the one you try to make, despite your experience.

Living <u>is</u> difficult,
for, unless you stay at home,
you are beset by danger and difficulty on all sides.
Even at home, and alone, you will face difficulties:
Some would say, far greater ones than you would ever face outside.

Yes, life is difficult,
and it is also mortal,
for everyone is born to die.

If your life is spent merely protecting yourself from death and difficulty,
Then your life is more than difficult –
it is <u>impossible,</u>
for you have set yourself a task at which you can never succeed –
and you will have made yourself afraid of life itself.

So you must accept that life is difficult,
and this is the first step to freedom from fear.

FROM HEART AND SOUL

THE LOVE TREE

Written to highlight the similarities between the growth and development of a tree, and the transition from friendship into love.

Dispersed by the trees, their origins unknown,
secreted by squirrels, in holes in the ground,
at the mercy of the winds by which they are blown,
some lost, or hidden, never to be found.
Seeds are like impressions and chance encounters,
Filed in our memories, apparently forever lost,
Until that sudden, unasked-for reminder pounces,
As we strive to recall a stray thought from the past.

Safely preserved in the rich, fertile loam,
Nature's casket senses that the time is right.
The growing shoot departs its seedcase womb
And starts the journey to warmth and light.
Similarly, thoughts and feelings emerge into the light of day,
Their owners becoming aware of a chance for them to grow;
two people, unsure of what they should say,
but determining that they should impart what each needs to know.

The seedling emerges, and fights to survive
the diseases, and the wildlife that compete for its space –
many will fall along the way – only the strong will thrive
to complete the course, and win the race.
A friendship forms, which both will cherish,
Despite the problems and hazards that Life has in store.
The foolish turn their backs, their love doomed to perish;
The wise accept their prize, and seek for more.

John Marshall

From seedling, to sapling, and thence to a tree,
towering above all with its strength and grace –
a living statue, for all to see
the everlasting cycle of Nature in its place.
So true love will grow from friendship's seed
and be an example to all around
of how love is there for all who need,
and generate more love, as once it was formed.

FROM HEART AND SOUL

TIME WARP

Each second is as a minute in the time we are apart,
Each minute, an hour that I am away!

Each hour, another day with heavy heart,
More depressed than I care to say!

Each day I do not spend with you
Is a week of solitary confinement.

A week not holding you, feeling blue,
Like a month of endless torment!

That month, a year in isolation -
A year seems to be a decade of pain -

Decades turned into a millennium –
Striving to drive me insane!

And then, we are together, united once more –
Time stops, and we defy the laws of time.

Each breath bringing us closer than before,
In loving unity, our singularity is sublime!!

John Marshall

THE TRAGEDY THAT IS WAR

Sectarian war rips a country apart,
with former neighbours now mortal enemies for life.
After years of control, they couldn't wait to start
To destroy their country with bloodshed and strife.

They pursue their goal with unbounded zeal
as they bomb, and maim, and kill –
no thought for how the People feel;
no time to consider the Public will.

Beautiful cities and towns remain
as a legacy to their killing spree –
blemishing the land with an ugly stain,
justified by some in their fight to be 'free'.

Many soldiers are injured, man hundreds killed
as the war washes over them, and leaves them behind:
But at least <u>they</u> knew <u>their</u> blood might be spilled,
And accepted that risk in the depths of their minds.

The real casualties are those who have no control
over the fighting and killing, and the taking of land.
No-one asked for <u>their</u> views in an opinion poll,
Or planned the campaign on the show of <u>their</u> hand.

Instead, women and children are totally ignored –
treated as objects that get in the way;
killed in their homes by the warring horde,
or abandoned like a toy at the end of play.

FROM HEART AND SOUL

Left with appalling injuries, and a lack of care,
and the despair of being abandoned to their fate.
Many of them without a family with which to share
the dismal future the war seeks to create.

The civilised world stands by, in righteous shock,
and deplores the fate of a nation –
but disagreement and politics only serve to mock
the need to act for the victims' salvation.

Basic humanitarian rights are withheld and denied,
while nations' leaders discuss what should be done.
And all this time, while they cannot decide,
A tragedy develops as victims are left alone.

Simple aid is all they seek, or ask –
medicine, food, and Life's most basic needs.
That should not be such a difficult task,
provided the World just listens, and heeds.

To end a war is a worthy cause,
But that should not be the over-riding aim.
We should act to help, not hesitate and pause,
if we are to avoid inaction's shame.

John Marshall

BING THE MAGNIFICENT

'What on Earth is a Bing?' I hear you say,
As you see me with my latest book.
Shall I tell you? I think I may!
And I give you a knowing look.

You've obviously never hear of Bing,
So I feel I am obliged to expound.
Bing is not an object, not a thing –
For Bing, he is a hound!

Not just any hound, though, as you will see,
But a dog with brains and intellect.
A dog who can interact with you and me
And converse like you would not expect.

He lives with a family down Epping Forest way,
And stays with 'the old poop' quite frequently.
With Tim (the poop) he loves to walk and play,
But when there, he also studies philosophy.

For Bing is a curious and inquisitive lad,
And loves to talk with Tim of things
He sees and hears – of new ideas he's had,
And of the importance this new knowledge brings.

Bing has his own names for the things he sees –
'Buzzers' and 'whizzers' visit the flowers,
'Red chests' and 'black 'uns' are in the trees,
His names challenging our reasoning powers.

FROM HEART AND SOUL

Bing likes nothing better than a tasty snack –
(or two, or three or more!)
Bonios and such are just the crack,
Or anything else that comes to paw.

Edible chess is a game he would fancy,
With flavours to suit a discerning lad.
The 'old poop', poor chap, thinks this a little chancy,
But tries to please with whatever is to be had!

Forest walks are a regular thing,
As they follow the paths between the trees.
The 'old wheezer' is often left behind by Bing,
As he slows down, and starts to wheeze.

Patient as ever, the lad sits at his feet,
or explores the smells he finds all about –
Then, ever hopeful, hoping for a treat,
Nudges Guv's pocket with his snout.

Everything around him arouses his interest,
And sparks his quizzing mind -
Always asking questions in his quest
For answers to the puzzles he may find.

'Why do birds go away each year?'
'Why do the furry flouncers hide nuts in the ground?'
To him, sometimes, things are not quite clear,
Until his enquiries result in the answer found.

Yes, our Bing is a very special hound
And we love him very much.
He's the perfect company to have around
On woodland walks, and so forth, and such!

John Marshall

THE BLACK AND WHITE MINSTREL SHOW!

'OVERTURE AND BEGINNERS, PLEASE!' the cry rings out -
Backstage, the guys and gals wait in the wings.
Gone any nerves, or last-minute doubt –
Their sole objective to dance and sing.

Dancers' bodies, muscles toned,
Hours of rehearsals they had endured -
All notes and steps to perfection honed,
Now, a perfect performance ensured.

Greasepaint, eyelashes and make-up done,
in gowns and suits all neatly attired;
Choreography ensuring they would move as one,
They take their positions, as required.

An expectant pause, the house lights dim, then
The announcer's voice rings out, loud, but mellow –
'LADIES AND GENTLEMEN,
IT'S THE BLACK AND WHITE MINSTREL SHOW'.
The orchestra strikes up as the curtain lifts –
Minstrels and Toppers take the stage.
From that moment on, attention never shifts
As the audience take in the colourful image.

Beautiful gowns on every girl,
The boys all dressed in suits so fine –
Skirts and petticoats swish and twirl
As the dancers move in perfect time.

FROM HEART AND SOUL

As each routine reaches its close
The stage suddenly seems to clear -
But backstage, ordered chaos reigns for those
having minutes to change before they reappear.

Dresses off, new dresses donned,
Hairpieces changed to suit the need –
Makeup repaired as if by magic wand,
A miracle change, of necessity achieved.

The audience is oblivious to all this activity,
As the show, for them, continues unabated.
Juggling, comedy, speciality acts and classic variety
All perform their acts, with the next routine awaited.

Thus, the show continues, medley follows medley,
Colourful costume changes come and go –
Musical magic and dance continue steadily
Until the end of yet another stunning show.

Across the decades, on TV, and stage as well –
This tradition continues to entertain and thrill.
Generations to come will fall under the spell
Of classic entertainment – tire, they never will!

John Marshall

THE OLD MAN

written for the funeral of Neville King, ventriloquist and comedian.

Neville - The old man's voice now silent falls,
As your act is now billing in heavenly music halls;
Retirement comes his way at last,
As he looks back fondly on memories past.

But, for you, dear Nev, the act goes on –
Old fans will greet you, one by one.
No doubt some silent angel awaits your knee,
And for your voice to make everyone laugh with glee.

George will be waiting, with many an old friend;
He has a company there – on that you can depend!
Give them our love, each and every one,
And bask in the show that will go on and on.

Find your audience, and make them smile,
Break a leg, and have them rolling in the aisle!
Save some spots for the rest of the cast,
Until they join you there, at last.

FROM HEART AND SOUL

MOTORWAY MEETINGS

Networks of motorways, like ribbons entwined,
Cover the country like wedding veils;
Cars - foraging ants in endless trails,
Follow nose to tail on routes so well defined.

Anonymous drivers go their separate ways,
unknown to each other - uncaring, too.
But some, perhaps just a few,
Have better things to do with their days!

Lovers, safe in their anonymity,
Some openly, others not so indiscreet,
Seek a service area in which to meet,
Flaunting their love with impunity.

To most, just a place to stop and rest,
or attend to Nature's call -
But our Lovers, oblivious to all,
Are engaged in a more urgent quest.

Eyes gaze into eyes, hands holding tight,
Treasuring the moment, making it last.
Until, only too soon, their time is past,
leaving lingering memories of love's delight.

Sweet dreams, and a stolen moment,
Are all they have to share -
A lingering kiss, to show they care,
And to show their Love's intent.

John Marshall

Homeward bound, alone they drive,
Lost in thought, with heavy heart.
Dreading the time they spend apart,
Trusting true love will grow and thrive.

FROM HEART AND SOUL

THE OAK TREE

He stands alone, the old oak tree;
Isolated, and exposed to the wind and rain.
Alone on the hill, for all to see,
The seasons pass him by, again and again.

From his vantage point, he looks around
and watches the world pass him by –
from the smallest creatures that walk the ground,
to the birds and clouds that fill the sky.

His life is lived at a leisurely pace,
As he slowly grows, year by year.
His roots, the anchors that hold him in place,
his branches, a canopy, built tier upon tier.

The persistent wind affects the way he grows,
As it pushes on him, branch and trunk.
A one-sided assault, all the time it blows;
leaning him sideways, like a wayward drunk.

Each season dictates the clothes he will wear –
in summer, a cool coat to shade him, and those below;
in autumn, his coat removed, his arms are laid bare;
in winter, delicate whites from tip to toe.

But, in spring, a new wardrobe he wears instead,
as he gains a tailored suit of green.
With room for the growth that lies ahead,
He stands on high, proud to be, and be seen.

John Marshall

THESE THINGS YOU ARE...

You are my summer, and my fall,
My winter, and my spring –
Times when our love will grow, and stand so tall,
So that our hearts rejoice and sing.

You are my morning, and my afternoon,
My evening, and my night –
I watch, as you walk around the room,
And the sight of you fills me with delight.

You are my waking, and my sleeping,
You are there throughout my day –
With you, and of you, my heart is singing
Of more Love than words can say!

FROM HEART AND SOUL

THE N.H.S.

From the cradle to the grave –
a commitment to health and care;
a promise our politicians freely gave
of a welfare state, forever there.

No matter whether young or old.
Mentally ill, or chronically sick;
from deadly disease to the common cold,
from appendicitis to childhood colic.

A dentist, to help preserve and care for our teeth,
free medicine, no matter what the cost;
contraception for all – the pill and the sheath,
a hospital bed when it is needed the most.

Little by little, we have seen the service fade –
costs increase as bureaucracy grows.
Once strong, it is now feeble and decayed,
damaged by authorities, with each cut they impose.

Children who deserve the chance to live,
condemned by the cost of the treatment they need;
reliant on the money a charity may give –
dependent on their parents to beg and plead.

Old people now living beyond their years,
Living against their wishes, in indignity.
The mentally ill, released to live with their fears,
Unable to cope with advancing senility.

John Marshall

'From cradle to the grave' no longer applies –
The commitment is no longer there.
Promises broken, politicians ignore the cries
Of pain and suffering everywhere.

FROM HEART AND SOUL

OUR FATE-FULL LIVES

The memory of love is there to see –
The meeting that might, or might not, be –
Lives exist in parallel worlds,
Blissfully unaware of how fate unfurls.

Pure chance dictates whether or not we meet,
Whether hearts be empty, or complete.
In ignorance of the part it plays each day,
Insignificant chance will have it's way.

A random choice - (do this, do that) -
Can change two lives at the drop of a hat.
A moment's action, or inaction, without conscious thought,
The difference between that which happens, or that which ought.

In many ways, it seems we HAVE no choice,
Our conscious will an unheard voice.
The things that happen are meant to be,
The paths we take are never free.

We were always meant to share our life -
To be together, as husband and wife.
Our Love, and our lives, pre-ordained and planned,
As a monument that will forever stand.

John Marshall

POPPIES

A field of poppies, shining red,
A simple flower with petals spread.
A reminder of suffering in pointless war,
A reminder that there should be no more.

A memory of battles where blood was shed;
A token worn to honour the dead.
No politics or creed should taint this image;
Instead, accept this symbol of respectful homage.

Display this flower with respectful pride,
And stand with others, side by side.
Show the world how we honour sacrifice
By wearing this simple, poignant device.

Remember the Fallen on Armistice Day,
Stand, head bowed, and silently pray
That their sacrifice was not in vain -
Pray those horrors never return again.

FROM HEART AND SOUL

THE GRACEFUL SWAN

Graceful in flight, defying gravity with their size,
Beating, pushing, and sighing, held aloft on massive wings,
they travel purposefully and majestically across the skies,
the most beautiful and perfect of flying things.

Graceful on water, they float quietly on their course,
effortless in movement, both solemn and serene.
Unresting, cruising silently, drifting without pause,
except for the occasional rest for food, sleep, or feather-preen.

Graceful in numbers, they cruise in line astern,
like 'men-of-war' with sails full-spread.
As if into battle sailing, they tack and turn,
jibe, and reach, first losing way, then going full speed ahead.

Graceful in love, they faithfully pair;
Heads bobbing in time, they flirt and dance:
Their courtship a ballet for all to see,
Re-enforcing the bonds that cement their romance.

Graceful is the swan in all these ways;
graceful in movement and in form.
Graceful is the swan on summer days;
Graceful as the wind on ripened corn.

John Marshall

NOW AND FOREVER

When I'm with you,
eternity is a step away;
my love continues to grow,
with each passing day.

This treasure of love,
I cherish within my soul,
how much I love you...
you'll never really know.

You bring a joy to my heart
I've never felt before;
with each touch of your hand
I love you more and more.

Whenever we say goodbye,
whenever we part,
know I hold you dearly,
deep inside my heart.

So these seven words,
I pray you hold true,
'NOW and FOREVER, and ALWAYS,
I WILL LOVE YOU.'

FROM HEART AND SOUL

IF HEAVEN HAD A TELEPHONE

If Heaven had a telephone,
We would use it all the time –
But maybe the 'busy' tone
Would always be on that line!

Even better would be the Internet
To speed the words of Love –
Or Skype, even better yet,
To see our loved ones up above.

But maybe we are half way there,
In our wish to be in touch.
Our loved ones are already aware
Of how we miss them so much.

Perhaps science will grant us what we wish,
And open that two way line
And give a gift all would cherish –
Our loved ones back, yours, and mine.

John Marshall

A GENTLE WORD

A gentle word like a spark of light,
Illuminates my soul;
And as each sound goes deeper,
It's YOU that makes me whole

There is no corner, no dark place
that YOUR LOVE cannot fill;
And if the world starts causing waves,
It's your devotion that makes them still.

And yes, you always speak to me,
In sweet honesty and truth;
Your caring heart keeps out the rain,
YOUR LOVE, the ultimate roof.

So thank you, my Love, for being there,
For supporting me, my life;
I'll do the same for you, you know,
My Beautiful, Darling Wife.

FROM HEART AND SOUL

DREAMS

Dreams, those nebulous thoughts of our sub-conscious mind,
ephemeral and tenuous, they drift and flow –
thought processes, memories and hopes, all unrefined,
challenging and tantalising visions that come and go.

Dreams, where the problems of life cease to exist,
where the impossible becomes achievable, if but for a while –
where hopes come true, no wish dismissed,
where the unattainable comes closer, if still fragile.

Dreams, which reflect the undercurrents of your thought –
sometimes dark and brooding, filled with doom:
Dreams, which may mock and torment, and leave you distraught,
taking the light from your life, and leaving only gloom.

Dreams, where everything seems solid and real –
when all that is sensed is truly there.
A loved one you can hold, and touch, and feel –
when it is easy to show how much you care.

Dreams, where life, for good or bad, can have its day,
with moments of beauty, humour, sadness or pain,
a transient, fleeting world, destined never to stay;
a world which offers all, then snatches it back again.

John Marshall

LOVE IN MY HEART

I etched my love in the sand...
But the waves just washed it away!

I drew it in the sky, with clouds......
But the wind just blew it away!

I penned it in a poem....
But with time, ink just fades away!

So I will hold it in my heart....
Because there, it can forever stay!!

FROM HEART AND SOUL

THE DRAGON SLAYER

While working about twenty years ago in the police in Sussex, we had a new computerised messaging system installed. Prior to going live we were encouraged to 'instant message' any other police station in the force to become familiar with the system. I had a friend, a female police officer who was serving at Crawley, a very busy and high-crime area, with adjacent Gatwick airport…officers could be seconded at virtually no notice to serve for two years at the airport, not a popular posting. My friend and I started exchanging messages about this, which developed into a prose story about dragons (aircraft) and the dragons' lair (airport), the Ivory towers was a nickname for force HQ. We exchanged episodes of this saga over the course of a week of nights, and I later translated these into 'The Dragonslayer"

In an ancient and more angry place
there dwelt a brave and shining knight,
his job to guard the dragon's peace
with all his strength and might.

He upheld the laws in that pleasant land,
happy with the world and his work.
With little but his wits to hand,
his duty he would never shirk.

One day, the Baron some strangers met,
from a far and distant shore.
They saw that he was powerful, yet
decided he had need of more.

Magic machines they then installed,
which bestowed an all-seeing eye.
The local people were held enthralled
as their secrets were laid open to the sky.

John Marshall

The baron, pleased with his shining knight,
decided with him his magic gift to share.
He summoned him to come within his sight
to the Ivory Towers, and join him there.

The knight made haste to do as bid,
Spending many days away from home.
He faced the machines from which others hid,
and learned by rote from an epic tome.

The spells required he learned by heart,
and mastered their secret ways.
At last, for home he could depart,
without any further annoying delays.

Once home, he practiced his new-found art,
until sure he was in command.
Then came the day for him to start
to supervise the Baron's land.

One day, the knight's town was struck by fire,
and the baron told him what had come to pass.
To help the shining knight in that distant land,
he sent a manuscript, first class.

It set out how to quench the flames,
and told who should attend.
It gave a list of many names,
and had many numbers at the end.

Alas, that manuscript went astray,
for the machines were hard to use.
It went, instead, many miles away,
where no-one could it's meaning deduce.

FROM HEART AND SOUL

This second place was vast and barren,
a den of sin and vice.
Nearby dwelt many a fire-breathing dragon,
which demanded frequent sacrifice.

In order to placate the beasts,
and prevent that town's demise,
they held great sacrificial feasts
as the dragons filled the skies.

Townsfolk also worked as slaves
in the evil dragon's lair,
and panic flooded down in waves
on any who were summoned there.

There dwelt in that town a damsel fair,
also in the Baron's employ.
She worked close by, in much despair
when once she knew naught but joy.

The damsel read that errant scroll,
and was puzzled by its form.
Perhaps, if her sacrificial bell should toll,
the knight would help her weather the storm?

She too could use the great machines,
and she spoke direct to the shining knight.
To her, he seemed to answer dreams,
and was most suited to save her with his might.

The knight fell for her charm and wit,
and pledged to be her champion.
With many barriers between them yet,
fate had deemed they be as one.

John Marshall

He made it his duty to keep in touch,
so that his help was always near,
and he grew to love her very much,
as he banished all her fear.

Then came that dread and fateful day
when the damsel's hour grew close.
Realising death was not far away,
she spoke once more to the knight she chose.

She told him of the danger great,
and that her life was now in balance.
She begged him come and cheat her fate
at great speed, with his trusty lance.

How long would it take for him to arrive
at that distant and barren plain?
His greatest speed he would contrive,
but would he yet arrive in vain?

Meantime, reprieve came in another guise,
as the baron heard what was taking place.
The damsel was told to visit the One most wise
and to stay there many days.

She spent her time most sad at heart,
as she was missing her shining knight.
Would he leave her, and depart?
She rather feared he might!

She begged the baron to set her free,
to return from whence she came.
Her fear of dragons would always be,
but with no knight, no day was the same!

FROM HEART AND SOUL

She speedily rode to her distant land,
hoping to see her champion there.
But, alas, the dragons were close at hand,
and they carried her off to their evil lair.

Although terror tore at her very soul,
she left her scarf as a signal there,
that the knight would discover the dragons' goal,
and save her from her grave despair.

Would he take up arms, and come to her,
and rescue her, as once he vowed?
Or had her time at the Ivory tower
the knight's chivalrous instincts cowed?

The night, meanwhile, in his peaceful land,
had become distressed and worried.
No messages came from the damsel's hand,
and he feared she was in need.

He questioned the machines without a pause,
with all the commands he knew.
No news he heard from their memory stores,
and his worries grew and grew.

He knew a grave lot had befallen her,
and suspected the dragons were to blame.
He resolved to find their secret lair,
and defy their flesh-devouring flame.

His shining suit he went and got,
his helmet, shield and lance.
He placed them in his chariot,
and set out to take his chance.

John Marshall

His chariot was exceeding fast,
with red stripes and flashing lights,
so the time soon came, when, at last,
he drew near the dragons' heights.

So that his approach might silent be,
he left his chariot and walked on foot.
What on the ground ahead could he see?
He drew nearer to have a look.

A scarf! A message left for him?
It was the damsel's, that he knew.
Her secret password, fine and thin,
embroidered on it, was the clue.

The find spurred him to a quicker pace,
his mind determined to save his maid.
He suddenly reached the dreaded place,
but our hero was not the least afraid!

After searching long and hard around,
a secret tunnel caught his eye.
To inner halls it led, deep underground,
far from the sun and deep blue sky.

He started to follow the winding track,
down to the bowels of the earth.
The temperature rose, but he turned not back,
for he was of high and noble birth.

Ahead, he heard a roaring sound
which would have terrified lesser men,
but still he pushed on, underground,
until he reached a large cavern.

FROM HEART AND SOUL

This place was, in fact, the dragons' home,
where they snarled, and spewed out fire.
And in a corner, sad, alone,
was the damsel, his heart's desire!

She raised her eyes, and saw him there;
the clouds on her face departed.
Her eyes lit up, gone all despair,
as the knight towards her started.

Uncaring of the monsters all around,
he dashed up to give her aid.
and, in one swift move, his arms so stout
gathered her, and he for the tunnel made.

As they saw the light of day once more,
and breathed the sweet, refreshing air.
He saw the largest dragon skyward soar,
and turned to meet him there.

He bid her in his chariot hide,
and turned to face the beast.
His shield turned breath and flames aside
until the dragon's flames had ceased.

His eagle eye ran o'er its pelt,
and he saw an undefended spot.
With his lance a mighty blow he dealt -
straight to that evil heart it shot.

The dragon fell, its life blood gone,
in a ball of flame and smoke.
Tired, but happy, his battle won,
he cast aside his cloak.

John Marshall

He returned to where the damsel hid,
watching all that had taken place.
His arms around her he gently slid,
and he held her in a warm embrace.

He quietly smoothed away her fears,
stroked her hair, and wiped her face.
They shared a long and passionate kiss,
oblivious to that terrible place.

Never again would they be apart,
together would they stay -
forever in each other's heart
from that moment, until eternity.

They returned in joy to the Ivory towers
and told the Baron what had come to pass.
Their way was carpeted with flowers
and soft and lush green grass.

They wed in the sight of the great machines
as they gave their wedding oath.
They dreamed eternal, heavenly dreams,
and peace and happiness followed them both.

FROM HEART AND SOUL

FORGETTING TO REMEMBER

Written for Remembrance Day about five years ago

I remember my father when he told me of his war....
Of his worries and his fears while in a land so far away -
I remember his stories of the life he had before....
But I had forgotten, until I remembered, today.

I remember watching the newsreels, screened with pride,
Of war images, watched by millions so far away,
I remember the bombing, nightly defied,
But I had forgotten, until I remembered, today.

I remember Aden, The Gulf, Afghanistan....
The striving to give the innocent their say –
I remember Bosnia and The Falklands –
But I had forgotten, until I remembered, today.

I remember Vietnam, and Korea, too....
The Troubles, the bombings, the IRA –
I remember the soldiers who died for me and you,
But I had forgotten, until I remembered, today.

I remember Royal Wootton Bassett,
And those who stood in silence, along the way....
I remember our Forces, a National Asset,
But I had forgotten, until I remembered, today.

REMEMBER NOT TO FORGET!

John Marshall

LOVE IS THE GREATEST FEELING

Love is the greatest feeling,
Love is like a play,
Love is what I feel for you,
Each and every day,
Love is like a smile,
Love is like a song,
Love is a great emotion,
That keeps us going strong,
I love you with my heart,
My body and my soul,
I love the way I keep loving,
A love I can't control,
So remember when your eyes meet mine,
I love you with all my heart,
And I have poured my entire soul into you,
Right from the very start.

FROM HEART AND SOUL

A FLIGHT FROM NOWHERE

Written at the request of a friend (he wishes to remain nameless, but knows who he is!) as a tribute to his son, who from an early age had dreams of being a pilot, and with the help of his parents, and his own hard work, achieved his goal.

We all know that little boys like to dream
of what adult life will bring –
One lad, at an early age, actually *knew*, it seems,
and, to achieve it, would do everything.
His dream was pursued against advice,
with only parents to offer the necessary support.
A wise choice of subjects will have to suffice
to achieve the goal that has long been sought.

His wish to fly was so deeply ingrained
that nothing ever stood in the way –
A pilot's licence was quickly attained,
with hours of fundraising providing the means to pay.
Boot sales and sponsorship played their part,
along with the taxi of mum and dad.
To provide the funds for the early start
family help and hard work was all he had.

That, and determination to achieve his goal,
set him on the way to his flying career.
With a university degree and strength of soul
his course was set, firm and clear.
After a Services life of eighteen years,
rising quickly through the ranks,
his love of flying never disappears,
and civilian flying is now pursued with thanks.

John Marshall

The moral of this little poem is plain –
no matter the background, any dream you may achieve.
With love and support, any young person can attain
their heart's desire, through hard work and self-belief.

FROM HEART AND SOUL

TUNNEL TERRORISM

written just before the Channel Tunnel opened, the terrorist threat in Northern Ireland was very much still a problem, and I had a dream involving a terrorist attack on the tunnel.

Networks feeding,
Trains speeding,
Aiming for the tunnel's mouth;
Goods converging,
Passengers merging,
By road and rail, all heading south.

Tunnels winding,
Two countries binding,
Deep beneath the sea;
Tunnels slinking,
The countries linking,
A symbol of new unity.

Coaches packed,
Luggage stacked,
A family, sat in their car;
A truck loaded -
Unexpectedly exploded
By command transmitted from afar.
The noise first deafens,
Then, as suddenly, lessens,
'Til all is deathly still;
The screams of pain,
Again, and again,
Piercing, pleading, begging, shrill.

John Marshall

Twisted metal snares -
The remains of chairs
Imprisoning those who would survive;
Glass fragments spearing,
Growing flames searing,
Entombing, dismembering, burning them alive.

Then, water submerges,
Cleans, and purges,
And all becomes still once more;
Bodies floating,
With gases bloating,
As witness to this act of war.

The terrorist slaughters! -
Parents, sons and daughters -
He cares not who he kills;
His murdering mind
Cannot be confined -
To him, but an act of Political wills.

In the name of Unity,
He kills with impunity,
Not caring who is hurt on the way.
In the name of Religion
He creates division,
Pushing his declared objective yet further away.

There must be a solution,
And an end to revolution,
And a return to peaceful ways;
A return to humanity -
A return to sanity -
Before Mankind will see better days.

FROM HEART AND SOUL

LOVE, AS ART DISPLAYED

As a delicate insect in clearest amber bound,
Preserved on view for all eternity,
So my Love and adoration for you is found;
Held on view for the world to see.

As a work of art, in a gallery displayed,
A masterpiece in shape and style -
True Love, in classic form, portrayed
On view, yet growing all the while!

As a majestic building designed by Wren,
With soaring, vaulted arches spread,
Our hopes and dreams amongst them, then –
Freed from the cells of our confining heads.

As open as panoramic countryside,
Fresh air and wind blowing free –
A Love that never will be denied,
The Love that is You and Me.

The minute facets of the way I care,
The respect in which you're held,
Are placed in my heart, encapsulated there,
As our two lives into one strive to meld.

My Love for you I wear on my sleeve,
For all to see, and to know!
Be assured, that Love will never leave,
Just as I will never go!

John Marshall

Just Love me, sweet, as I Love you,
And hold me in your heart –
For then, what we have is Good and True,
And we will truly never be apart!

FROM HEART AND SOUL

THE ETERNAL MOON

New moon, that silver strand just coming into sight,
The promise of renewal fulfilled once more –
The still-hidden face, looking shyly to the right,
as if forgetful of the many times that have gone before.

Still lacking power, she gathers strength, night by night,
As more and more comes into view –
scudding clouds still hiding her pubescent light,
still lacking the strength to push its way through.

Full moon, that radiant orb, displaying all her glory,
its presence affecting the World for good or bad –
always in Mankind's developing story,
bringing romance to some, turning others mad.

With a soft, white gaze, she looks on all below;
A silvery, sea-surface sheen spreading serenity –
Imbuing lovers the World across with its gentle glow,
A symbol of Love's constancy, for all eternity.

Old moon, the power fading rapidly away, as if by theft,
As she prepares to leave us all behind;
 turning her back, as her face turns left,
she disappears, but will never desert Mankind.

For half her life, she is never seen,
As she hides herself from all below.
But she will return, her promise to redeem,
To watch over us, and protect us as we grow.

John Marshall

LOVE DEFINED

To love is to share life together -
to build special plans just for two -
to work side by side,
and then smile with pride,
as, one by one, those dreams come true.

To love is to help and encourage,
with smiles and sincere words of praise;
to take time to share,
to listen and care,
in tender, affectionate ways.

To love is to have someone special -
one on whom you can always depend;
to be there through the years,
sharing laughter and tears,
as a partner, a lover, a friend.

To love is to make special memories
of moments you love to recall;
of all the good things
that sharing life brings,
love is the greatest of all.
We've learned the full meaning
of sharing and caring,
and having our dreams all come true;
We've learned the full meaning
of being in love
by being and loving together.

FROM HEART AND SOUL

WHAT IS LOVE?

What is love but an emotion,
So strong and so pure,
That nurtured and shared with another
All tests it will endure?

What is love, but a force
To bring the mighty low,
With the strength to shame the mountains
And halt time's ceaseless flow?

What is love, but a triumph,
A glorious goal attained,
The union of two souls, two hearts
A bond the angels have ordained?

What is love, but a champion,
To cast the tyrant from his throne,
And raise the flag of truth and peace,
And fear of death o'erthrow?

What is love, but a beacon,
To guide the wayward heart,
A blazing light upon the shoals
That dash cherished dreams apart?

And what is love, but forever,
Eternal and sincere,
A flame that through wax and wane
Will outlive life's brief years?

John Marshall

So I'll tell it on the mountaintops,
In all places high and low,
That love for you is my reason to be,
And will never break or bow.
'Forever And Always,
I Will Love You.'

FROM HEART AND SOUL

THE VALUE OF INDEPENDENCE

Freedom and independence, two possessions we treasure
in varying degrees as through Life we go –
some consider their importance to be of equal measure –
some are unfortunate in never having the chance to know.

But though both may seem to be entwined, hand in hand,
in truth, this is not always the case.
Perhaps, when freedom is the goal for which you have planned,
you may feel lack of Independence puts you back in your place.

Freedom is the ability to go where you choose,
with whom, and whenever, you care –
to plan, and to dream, with no-one to refuse
their consent, thus casting you into despair.

But, without independence, freedom is but a hollow shell,
that unreachable goal that taunts from afar –
its lack casts a shadow, like an overpowering spell,
preventing you from following your own guiding star.

Independence is the key that unlocks freedom's gate,
and opens up your path to the future.
It permits you to decide and control your fate,
giving it full meaning and measure.

ABOUT THE AUTHOR

Starting life in South Yorkshire, after a 'normal' education to High School level, John joined the Police Cadets, and after three years of training and introduction to the Police world, he completed his training as a Police Constable, and was posted to a number of mining villages in South Yorkshire, before voluntarily transferring to Sussex, where he was posted to Rye, a beautiful 12th century market town close to the Kent border. His duties there included foot patrol around the town, and later as crew of the Sub Divisional response car, still working from Rye.

In the summer of 1983 he successfully applied for the post of village bobby in one of the village beats within Rye Sub Division, responsible for a number of villages covered by three different parish councils, and including a stretch of the Channel coast, and a coastal country park at Fairlight, just outside Hastings.

This idyllic life was interrupted in the autumn of 1984 by two major events. He was on duty for the Conservative Party conference in Brighton, when the Grand Hotel was bombed by the IRA. Shortly afterwards, for about a year, he found himself covering the miners' strike in various locations around the UK.

Towards the end of his service, he became involved in tutoring newly-appointed police constables, and then, on a monthly basis as an assessor, involved in the selection of potential recruits applying to join the Force. He also became involved in the training of Special Constables, and in the running and training of his Station's Police Cadet unit (See the poem - *A Jubilee Walk*!)

On retirement in 1999 he toured Europe in an American motor home, before settling with his wife Dorothy in rural Shropshire.

ABOUT THE PUBLISHERS

Saron Publishers has been in existence for about ten years, producing niche magazines. Our first venture into books took place in 2016 when we published *The Meanderings of Bing* by Tim Harnden-Taylor. *The Ramblings of Bing* came out in time for Christmas 2017. *Minstrel Magic* by Eleanor Pritchard was published in June 2017 and tells the phenomenal show business story of the George Mitchell Singers and the Black and White Minstrels. Further publications in 2017 included *Penthusiasm*, a collection of short stories and poems from a writing group based in the beautiful town of Usk. 2018 started with *Every Woman Remembered*, the story of the Newport women who lost their lives in the First World War, and will end with a collaboration with Caerleon schoolchildren to mark the centenary of the end of that war. There'll be lots more in between too.

Join our mailing list by emailing info@saronpublishers.co.uk. We promise no spam.

Visit our website saronpublishers.co.uk to keep up to date and to read reviews of what we've been reading and enjoying.

Follow us on Facebook @saronpublishers.

Follow us on Twitter @saronpublishers.

www.ingramcontent.com/pod-product-compliance
Lightning Source LLC
Chambersburg PA
CBHW020429010526
44118CB00010B/501